ALL RIG

MW00620171

Sans Merci
© 2009, Johnna Adams
Trade Edition, 2013
Cover image by: Lindsay Moore
Contact: lovemefondue@yahoo.com
ISBN 978-1-934962-46-6

Militant Language
a play with sand
by Sean Christopher Lewis
5 Males, 1 Female

Synopsis: Set in modern Iraq, this savage contemporary fable ignites when a pair of American soldiers return from a routine surveillance detail covered in blood. The barracks are no safe haven. The Captain fights to control his troops as they walk the high-wires of a secret homosexual affair, the sexual abuse of a female soldier, a missing Iraqi boy, and a baby found in the desert, ala Moses. This play explores how violence begets violence, lies beget lies, truth is born from trust, and understanding war makes as much sense as sand raining from the heavens.

The Sacred Geometry of S&M Porn
by Johnna Adams
16 Actors playing various roles

Synopsis: A troubled young man with a stack of dirty magazines + a dead woman stealing souls + a televangelist grilled by Mike Wallace + a whore seeking enlightenment + a disgruntled woman wielding a gun = an assassination plot, weird sex, the Crystal Cathedral, a whole lotta money and a new religion.

Contains nudity and adult subject matter

SANS MERCI

By Johnna Adams

SANS MERCI was first produced by the Bloomington Playwrights Project, Bloomington, Indiana, October 23 – November 8, 2008 as the winner of the Bloomington Playwrights Project's 2008-2009 Reva Shiner Award. The world premiere production was directed by Bruce Burgun. The cast and crew were as follows:

Kelly - Margot Morgan
Elizabeth - Francesca Sobrer
Tracy - Molly Kruse

Stage Manager - Amy Moon
Set Designer - Lee Burckes
Light Designer - Lee Burckes
Set Painter - Lora Conrad
Costume Advisor - Alexandra Morphet
Dresser - Jack Johnson
Props Master - Avery Wigglesworth

SANS MERCI was first produced in New York by Flux Theatre Ensemble, August Schulenburg, Artistic Director, at the Fourth Street Theatre, April 26 – May 17, 2013. The New York premiere was directed by Heather Cohn. The cast and crew were as follows:

Kelly - Rachael Hip-Flores
Elizabeth - Susan Ferrara
Tracy - Alisha Spielmann

Stage Manager - Audrey Marshall
Scene Designer - Charles Murdock Lucas
Sound Designer - Janie Bullard
Lighting Designer, Prod. Mgr. - Kia Rogers
Technical Director - Matt Vieira
Costume Designer - Will Lowry
Props Master - Sara Slagle
PR Press Rep - Emily Owens

Characters

KELLY, mid-20s
ELIZABETH, 50s
TRACY, early-20s

Settings
KELLY's Los Angeles apartment. Also a lecture hall, hallway, and dorm room at the University of California at Irvine. The "Cliffs of Glory" in Colombia.

Time
The present and three years in the past.

Playwright's Note
When a character name is followed by an ellipsis, as such:

KELLY: . . . .

The author is indicating a non-verbal response to the previous line. The ellipsis line may be played in many ways: as a pause, a beat, a look, a movement, a silence, a smile, a sudden thought, or it can just be used to give the scene some air, some room, some tension, etc.

When several ellipses lines are strung together it is helpful to think of them as bouncing non-verbal responses, e.g., one character shrugs another character reacts to the shrug with a toss of her head.

A slash (/) in the middle of a character's line indicates an interruption. The next speaking character should begin her line where the slash appears.

SANS MERCI

1. ALONE AND PALELY LOITERING

KELLY lies on her couch. She wears a headset and listens to an MP3 player. She is not listening to music. She has been crying and is in a mellow, sad mood. Her jeans are unfastened. Occasionally she places a hand between her legs and rubs herself very casually. She does not have the energy to masturbate, but touches herself languidly as she listens.

A cane is propped against the side of the couch.

She lives in a one bedroom apartment in Los Angeles. We see her living room and small kitchen. Books and magazines are stacked along all the available walls. There are a few literature books, but most of the titles are history, political science, current events, conspiracy theory, eastern religion, atlases, reference books, and biography. The magazines are National Geographic, Mother Jones, Yoga Journals, Utne Reader, etc. There are also a few plants, a poster of Cesar Chavez, a photo of Lech Walesa at the Gdansk strike, photos from Abu Ghraib, drawings of Babaji, and a series of large photos of Rachel Corrie. She has a bulletin board with a world map with pins marking Amnesty International human rights violations.

Near the couch there is a small Ikea computer desk with a laptop. The rest of the furniture includes some canvas folding chairs, thrift store bar stools, and a small TV on one of the shelves. There is a kitchen counter that serves as a dining area.

In the kitchen, her food is mostly health food stuff from Whole Foods. There are also raw food recipe books and a shelf of herbs, sprouts, fresh fruits, and vegetables. Her dishes are done and on the drying rack.

A large window at the back of her apartment overlooks the apartment complex's central courtyard. She lives in a typical Los Angeles motel-style apartment building with about twenty units. It is uncharacteristically over-cast and rain pours down outside.

After the house lights go down, through the window, we see ELIZABETH enter the apartment complex. She wears an orange rain poncho thrown over her conservative clothes. She carries a large handbag and a red umbrella. She consults a piece of paper and looks at the door numbers on the apartments. She finds KELLY's apartment and knocks on the door.

KELLY is startled out of her reverie. She fastens her pants, guiltily, retrieves her cane, and goes to look out the window. ELIZABETH waves at her uncertainly. KELLY puts the MP3 player in a desk drawer and opens the front door.

KELLY: Yes?

ELIZABETH: Is this your usual weather? I'm about to build an ark.

KELLY: It's not usual. No.

ELIZABETH: I thought LA was supposed to be sunny.

KELLY: Can I help you?

ELIZABETH: Someone up there must have known I was coming and sent the storm clouds in ahead of me.

KELLY: Are you looking for someone?

ELIZABETH: Yes.

KELLY: Who are you looking for?

ELIZABETH: Do you know your neighbors?

KELLY: No.

ELIZABETH: So, you wouldn't recognize a name, would you?

KELLY: I guess not.

ELIZABETH: I think that's a generational thing. No one your age knows your neighbors. Everyone my age wishes we didn't know our neighbors. Maybe that's evolution at work. A smartening up of the species.

KELLY: I could help you find the apartment number at least.

ELIZABETH: I have the right apartment. I'm looking for you, Kelly.

KELLY: . . .

ELIZABETH: . . .

KELLY: Do I know you?

ELIZABETH: We've never met. But we've spoken on the phone. Once or twice.

KELLY: Oh?

ELIZABETH: I'm from Chicago. I'm Elizabeth Bird.

KELLY: . . .

ELIZABETH: . . .

KELLY: You're Tracy's mom.

ELIZABETH: I'm Tracy's mom.

KELLY: . . .

ELIZABETH: . . .

KELLY: Come in.

(ELIZABETH leaves her soaking umbrella outside. She removes the poncho and leaves it next to the umbrella. She enters the apartment.)

ELIZABETH: I had to buy a rain poncho at a gas station. And an umbrella. I certainly didn't pack for all this. My husband asked if I was taking a bathing suit. I told him I wasn't going to the beach, for heaven's sake. But with this rain, maybe I should have brought a bathing suit. Maybe a scuba diving suit. . . . . It's colder than I expected, too.

KELLY: . . .

ELIZABETH: . . .

KELLY: It gets chilly at night. It's been cold during the day lately, too.

ELIZABETH: Well, Los Angeles certainly lies to the rest of the nation, then, with all the bragging about 70 degree weather year-round.

KELLY: It gets a little colder than that sometimes.

ELIZABETH: . . .

KELLY: How did you get my address? I've moved.

ELIZABETH: Your parents sent flowers to the memorial service. I had their address. And I sent a thank you card. For the flowers.

KELLY: That was . . . that was nice of you.

ELIZABETH: And I called them. They gave me your phone number and your address.

KELLY: That's good.

ELIZABETH: Yes.

KELLY: . . .

ELIZABETH: I was going to call you. But, I thought, no. Not just out of the blue. That might be jarring. So I thought, why not take a day and just go out there? Come see you instead. We never got to meet. . . . My husband just said, "Take a bathing suit." So you can see what his attitude is. Mr. Sarcasm. So I thought . . . why not? . . . . You live your whole life by these little rules. Call and don't just drop by. But you don't know

11

why. Rules are supposed to keep people safe, but they never do. No one is safe. . . . .So, I hoped this would be easier. For you. For us both..

KELLY: Sure. Can I get you something?

ELIZABETH: That's very polite. No. I'm fine. Sorry.

KELLY: I have herbal tea.

ELIZABETH: No. Don't feel like you have to . . . to entertain. I just-- . . . Well. . . . You know. . . .We never met.

KELLY: I know. I feel bad about that. I wanted to go to the memorial in Chicago. But. . . I was sort of . . . I was out of it.

ELIZABETH: Well, you had a memorial here. At the university.

KELLY: We did.

ELIZABETH: I wanted to come to that. So did my husband. But I was sort of out of it, too. I was hospitalized. For four months. Tranquilized. I'm not sure I was even aware it was happening.

KELLY: . . .

ELIZABETH: . . .

KELLY: I'm sorry.

ELIZABETH: Maybe I'll have some herbal tea. If you're offering.

KELLY: Chamomile?

ELIZABETH: Good.

KELLY: I make that well. I buy the little flowers. And use a french press.

(KELLY washes her hands. She gets a pitcher of filtered water from the fridge and puts a glass container of chamomile flowers on the kitchen counter.)

ELIZABETH: Fancy. I just use Lipton's for tea. And I never have any in the house. We're coffee drinkers. Bill, that's my husband, practically tithes to Starbucks. Their stock goes down, they call our house and say "Mr. Bird, have we offended you? What have we done? How can we atone?" If they made IV packs with the little green mermaid, he'd buy them. I call that little green mermaid "the other woman." . . . . Well. . . . . Did Tracy like tea made from flowers? When you lived together?

KELLY: She drank it. She liked it.

ELIZABETH: She never drank it at home. She never asked for any. I would have gotten it for her. . . . So, you have a new job? Right? That's what your mother said.

KELLY: I work for a non-profit. The Foundation Center. We help people find and apply for grants. I'm a grant writer.

ELIZABETH: Fantastic! That must be good work. Meaningful.

KELLY: I guess.

ELIZABETH: Yeah. Sure. You're one of those people. Who do meaningful work. And love what they do. One of those lucky people.

KELLY: I'm just getting started.

ELIZABETH: Yeah. Sure. But you're one of the lucky ones that gets to do what she wants. Good for you! Do you see your folks a lot?

KELLY: I don't.

ELIZABETH: You don't get up to San Francisco to see them?

KELLY: Not often.

ELIZABETH: What is it? A six hour drive?

KELLY: I just don't get up there much.

ELIZABETH: Holidays?

KELLY: Some.

ELIZABETH: But not much?

KELLY: I don't get along well. With my dad. With my brothers. There are fights. So I don't go.

ELIZABETH: Oh. . . . . Well, I talked to your mother. She seemed nice.

KELLY: She is. Sometimes she comes here.

ELIZABETH: Well, that's good. It's good you get along with your mother.

KELLY: . . .

ELIZABETH: Tracy and I always got along. Some mothers and daughters, you know, when the girl hits a certain age, they just don't get along. But we always hit it off pretty well. No fireworks. . . . Right up to college, she talked to me all the time. About anything. About boys. About who drank, who did drugs at her school. If she'd gone to school near home, I bet we'd still talk. She could never hide anything from me.

KELLY: She was very open.

ELIZABETH: . . .

KELLY: . . .

ELIZABETH: Yes.

KELLY: She told me that you always got along. Always could talk.

ELIZABETH: Good. I hoped she knew that. . . . You two met in a literature class?

KELLY: Feminist Studies in Art and Literature.

ELIZABETH: Was that it?

KELLY: She did a presentation. On Keats.

ELIZABETH: Keats! . . . I loved Keats. I was a literature major. I taught Keats. When I got my masters degree,

I taught Keats to undergraduates. Tracy: grew up with Keats. He was like a godfather.

KELLY: Yes. She told me.

ELIZABETH: What poem?

KELLY: It was on *La Belle Dame Sans Merci*.

ELIZABETH:
I met a lady in the meads,
Full beautiful - a faery's child,
Her hair was long, her foot was light,
And her eyes were wild.

KELLY: Right.

ELIZABETH: Beautiful. . . .

KELLY: It was.

ELIZABETH: My nieces and nephews can quote long passages from Quentin Tarantino. I know Keats. Another generational thing. Not an evolutionary advancement this time.

KELLY: Probably not.

ELIZABETH: So that's feminist literature now. Well, why not? She keeps knights as slaves, doesn't she? *La Belle Dame Sans Merci*? That's what the feminists all really want. Feminism at its core is more about female superiority than equality.

KELLY: That's very post-modern of you.

ELIZABETH: Is it?

KELLY: I don't think Tracy: could quote Quentin Tarantino. But she had the Keats' poem memorized.

ELIZABETH: She was an exception. A throwback. Keats stole the title for *La Belle Dame Sans Merci* from a French poem from the 14th or 15th century. Alain Chartier. Chartier's poem was about a man with a dead lover. Very different. Very sad.

I leave it to the lover, who nurses
Hopes that his wound might heal,
To make ballads, songs and verses,
That each might his own skill reveal.
My lady, by her will, did steal
At her Death, God save her soul,
And carry away, my power to feel,
That lies with her beneath the stone.

KELLY: . . .

ELIZABETH: . . .

KELLY: . . .

ELIZABETH: And how do you like your new apartment?

KELLY: It's good.

ELIZABETH: Good. This is your first apartment? The first place you've lived since the dorms at UCI?

KELLY: No. The third.

ELIZABETH: Goodness. You move around a lot. . . Three apartments in three years. It's like someone's chasing you. Have you been at the same job since college?

KELLY: No. I've had several.

ELIZABETH: Well, that's no good.

KELLY: Look, Mrs. Bird—

ELIZABETH: Oh, Liz. Please. Liz.

KELLY: Did you come all this way just to-- . . . .?

ELIZABETH: Just to meet you. Just to talk with you. To see you. . . . Tracy really admired you. I know that from the way she spoke about you. The e-mails she wrote me. The phone calls.

(KELLY sets the tea kettle on the stove. She takes a french press from a cabinet and fills the reservoir with chamomile flowers. She spills some on the counter.)

KELLY: Look. I have to meet someone . . . a co-worker... for dinner tonight. Some stupid thing, So I don't have much time right now.

ELIZABETH: Sure. Can I help you with that?

KELLY: No. I can manage. If you want to set something up—we could set up a time—maybe tomorrow—

ELIZABETH: It must be difficult learning to do things with that cane.

KELLY: . . .

ELIZABETH: . . .

KELLY: It's fine.

ELIZABETH: Will it get better? Your leg?

KELLY: . . .

ELIZABETH: . . .

KELLY: No. It won't.

ELIZABETH: I'm sorry. I think I read that you'd been injured. Some newspaper article about what happened. But, it really didn't register. I didn't know how serious it was. I'm sorry—

KELLY: Maybe we can have lunch someplace. Tomorrow. I know a nice restaurant on Santa Monica Boulevard. Hugo's. It's all organic. They do a nice lunch or brunch.

ELIZABETH: I fly out tonight.

KELLY: Oh. When did you get in?

ELIZABETH: This morning. If you only have a half hour now, that would be fine.

(KELLY takes two mugs from a cabinet and sets them on the counter.)

KELLY: Okay.

ELIZABETH: Thank you.

KELLY: I don't mean to be short with you. I don't mean to be unkind.

ELIZABETH: I understand.

KELLY: It's not that I don't want to talk to you.

ELIZABETH: I surprised you. I gave you no warning.

KELLY: It's been hard for me, too.

ELIZABETH: I'm sure.

KELLY: . . .

ELIZABETH: . . .

KELLY: What did you want to know?

ELIZABETH: Well, most of our information about what happened came to us second- or third-hand. . . . We did eventually get her body back. In a sealed casket. The mortician said I didn't want to see it, and I didn't argue. I was probably taking two valiums an hour then. It's a wonder I'm not dead. So, I never saw her body. We got a box of her things. From the university. From someone named Tiffany.

KELLY: She was our RA. At the dorm.

ELIZABETH: Well, she sent me Tracy's things from your dorm room. I suppose you were still in the hospital.

KELLY: Yes. Her things were gone when I got out.

ELIZABETH: But, we never got her passport. Or her wallet. Or her jewelry. The things she took to Colombia. Those things. I thought you might have them.

KELLY: I do.

ELIZABETH: Can I have her things, please?

KELLY: . . .

ELIZABETH: . . .

KELLY: All of them?

ELIZABETH: Whatever you have. You have all of her things from Colombia?

KELLY: Yes.

ELIZABETH: Those are the things I want, then. If it isn't too much trouble.

KELLY: . . .

ELIZABETH: . . . .

(KELLY goes to the bedroom door.)

ELIZABETH: And there was something else.

(ELIZABETH pulls a flag out of her handbag. It is a pride flag. Her hands shake.)

ELIZABETH: *(CONT.)* This was in the box the girl from the university sent us. This flag. It was in a smaller box. labeled "things hanging on her wall." It's a pride flag, I think.

KELLY: Yes. I remember it.

ELIZABETH: It's unfamiliar to me. I don't know why she had it. And I wanted to ask you about it.

KELLY: . . .

ELIZABETH: I wanted to ask you about this.

KELLY: . . .

ELIZABETH: . . .

KELLY: I have her backpack. I have the clothes she was wearing. The clothes they cut off her when they raped us. I have her last journal. Those are the things I have. I'll get them.

ELIZABETH: I want to ask you if you and Tracy were lovers.

2. OH WHAT CAN AIL THEE, KNIGHT-AT-ARMS?

Lights cross fade to TRACY, who stands at a lectern reading from a paper.

TRACY:
And there she lulled me asleep
And there I dreamed - Ah! woe betide! -
The latest dream I ever dreamt
On the cold hill side.
I saw pale kings and princes too,
Pale warriors, death-pale were they all;
They cried - 'La Belle Dame sans Merci
Hath thee in thrall!'

And in these lines Keats' true feminist perspective on *La Belle Dame sans Merci* is revealed. This fearsome faery's child has control over kings, princes, and strong warriors. She is siren-like. She has realized her dormant matriarchal destiny and rules rulers. It is not explained to the reader what the engine of her power is. We aren't sure if it is her beauty that captures men, or some strange influence beyond mortal understanding. The title, if translated from modern French, says that the beautiful lady is without thanks. Thankless. But, Keats stole the title from Alain Chartier's 15th century poem by the same name. And in Chartier's time, the word *merci* meant something closer to our modern English word mercy. Or pity. So she is a beautiful woman without mercy, without pity for the men she enslaves.

In Keats' day, women were the enthralled sex. Chained to husband and children. Trapped by societal constraints. Trapped, perhaps, by their own capacity for mercy. Because they pitied the loving husband and the needful children who depended on them to wear their domestic chains. But Keats' creation, his faery-child, has thrown off all constraints. She is not burdened with pity or remorse like mortal women. She is free. She has escaped the woman's trap of empathic reverie. She never feels the pain of people who are hungry, who are hurting, who are in desperate need. She can watch all our suffering with cool detachment. She is godlike in this. Stanza eight:

She took me to her elfin grot,
And there she wept and sighed full sore,
And there I shut her wild wild eyes
With kisses four.

Perhaps the most beautiful line in the poem. *And then I shut her wild wild eyes.* Her eyes are wild because that is the opposite of civilized. And the civilized woman is conditioned to have mercy. To feel pity. Even to wallow in those feelings. Only the wild soul is free of the trap of compassion.

La Belle Dame sans Merci is so powerful, so compelling, so utterly impartial, she may not be a woman at all. Keats may, in fact, be using her as a metaphor for the world. *La Belle Dame sans Merci* may be the mother earth, which has no mercy for her children. She is impartial with her floods, her earthquakes, her hurricanes, her destructive powers. Or perhaps *La Belle Dame sans Merci* is human civilization which is so cruel at times it seems designed to thwart humans rather than advance--

(TRACY breaks off. She is trembling.)

TRACY *(CONT.)*: I'm sorry. . . I'm sorry. I seem to be having a panic attack. I stayed up all night. And I wanted to do Keats justice, and I think I'm-- . . I'm having a panic attack. Professor McDonaugh, I'm sorry. I just need- . . . . I'm so sorry. I need some air.

(TRACY runs from the lectern. She flees to a hallway, where she crumples to the ground, hyperventilating. KELLY runs into the hallway from the classroom. She carries a backpack.)

KELLY: Okay. . . It's all right. You're going to be all right. . . Put your head between your knees, okay? Just think about breathing. If you need to start sobbing or something, just do it. Okay? Just let it out. It might help you breathe. Don't worry about anyone in there. It's not important.

TRACY: Oh god.

KELLY: It's all right. You're going to be okay.

TRACY: I can't breathe.

KELLY: You're hyperventilating. Put your head between your knees. . . There. Just think about breathing.

TRACY: I'm so stupid.

KELLY: Hey. You are not.

(TRACY slowly starts to breathe.)

TRACY: So stupid.

KELLY: Your presentation was the only one I actually listened to. You sounded like you really knew what you were talking about. It was good.

TRACY: I'm p-panicking.

KELLY: Just breathe.

(They breathe together. KELLY puts her hand on TRACY's back. TRACY calms a bit.)

TRACY: You-- . . you really liked it?

KELLY: Are you kidding? That was amazing. It wasn't even like you were talking about a poem. It was like you were talking about a loved one. It was great.

TRACY: My mom-- . . .

KELLY: Yeah?

TRACY: Read me Keats. When I was little. *(gasps)* I just wanted to do him justice.

KELLY: You did. You were amazing. I didn't get all that from that poem. You're really smart, you know. You should speak up more in class. I don't think I heard you say anything before this. I was surprised. I didn't know you had all that in you.

TRACY: If I speak up-- . . . . Oh, god.

KELLY: Yeah. If you speak up?

TRACY: This might happen. Again. Panic.

KELLY: You're scared of speaking in public? You shouldn't be. You speak very well.

TRACY: That's not it. I don't mind the speaking. It's just— . . . It's irrational. It's like people who are scared of heights. Most of the time they aren't scared of falling. They're scared of jumping. And that's what makes me panic. It's not that I mind speaking and messing up and looking stupid. That would be rational. I get panicked because I'm afraid the words might jump. And I might suddenly be talking about this fantasy life I had about emigrating to Mars when I was twelve and having my first sexual experience with green scaled hermaphrodites, or start confessing to some sort of sexual attraction to small Asian children that I don't feel, or just start screaming and begging the universe for a mercy it is incapable of showing. I'm just afraid the words are going to jump. From my mouth. And I won't be able to stop it until the people in the room rise up and stone me to death like biblical peasants. It's irrational. But it's really strong.

KELLY: Well, I think you got your breath back.

TRACY: *(laughs)* Yeah. . . Yeah.

KELLY: I think you're brave.

TRACY: If I were brave, I wouldn't be sitting on the floor struggling to breathe.

KELLY: Sometimes the attempt is enough. I really believe that. Here.

(KELLY takes a water bottle from her bag and hands it to TRACY. TRACY drinks.)

TRACY: Thanks. That's nice. You're nice. You're really being nice to me.

KELLY: Hey, I'm a fan now. Seriously. I liked the part where you said the poem might be a metaphor for the lack of mercy and pity in the world. I think the world looks that way to the poor and the hopeless and persecuted. Merciless.

TRACY: Yeah.

KELLY: So you really opened my eyes. To Keats.

TRACY: If I did, I'm glad. Because I love him. My mother has a degree in poetry. Almost a PhD. I was raised on Keats the way other kids were raised on Sesame Street. I love him.

KELLY: Are you a poetry major?

TRACY: Literature. What's your major?

KELLY: Political Sciences.

TRACY: You're going to be a politician?

KELLY: An activist. I already am, sort of.

TRACY: I've seen you in the student center. Passing out flyers for Amnesty International.

KELLY: Yeah. I'm going to Colombia this summer. To help the U'wa Indians.

TRACY: Are they starving?

KELLY: No. The Occidental Petroleum Corporation, a big psychotic US mega-corporation, is stealing their lands to extract fossil fuels. We're going to help them organize.

TRACY: Oh. Wow.

KELLY: Plan protests. Chain ourselves to some trees they want to bulldoze. I'm going with a camera crew.

TRACY: Is it dangerous?

KELLY: No. The U'wa reservation is surrounded by rebel forces. The rebel forces control almost half of Colombia right now. But they're on our side, and we have their permission to be there. They want US corporations to stop raping their lands, too.

TRACY: But you're risking your life. I mean, those rebels have guns. Something might happen.

KELLY: They would never kill US citizens.

TRACY: What do your parents think?

KELLY: I wanted to join the International Solidarity Movement and go to Palestine, like Rachel Corrie.

TRACY: Oh.

KELLY: And my parents didn't want that. So we compromised on this Colombia protest. I may still go to Palestine someday.

TRACY: You must be very passionate about . . . about injustice, I guess.

KELLY: I am. I can't sleep a lot because of it. And I feel guilty, you know? For having so much when others have so little.

TRACY: Do you have a boyfriend? What does he think about it?

KELLY: I don't have one.

TRACY: Oh.

KELLY: Don't let me talk your ear off about the U'was. I get crazy excited about it and go on and on.

TRACY: I think that's great. You're passionate about things. You can talk in front of class without experiencing a crippling fear that you will experience a total enema-like purging of the vocal chords all over the listeners. Oh god.

KELLY: I bet you still get an A when you hand in the written part.

TRACY: Professor McDonaugh hates me. She thinks I'm weak.

KELLY: She's weak! You should despise her. What the hell kind of Professor of Feminist Arts and Literature brings Harlequin Romance novels into class and reads them while the class takes pop quizzes?

TRACY: Isn't that weird? I thought that was weird, too.

KELLY: It's sick. The whole class is supposed to be about not buying into the male patriarchal fantasy of the goddamned subservient female sex object in literature and the arts. And she drags her over-permed, polyester wearing ass into class and *subverts* the entire curriculum by cracking the spine on something called *Burning Lust and Wanton Surrender*? While we're all being quizzed on the feminist perspective in early Renaissance drama? What? Huh?

TRACY: She is over-permed.

KELLY: It's like a French poodle fucked Elsa Lanchester's hair from bride of Frankenstein. Professor McDonaugh's hair is the love child.

TRACY: . . . . You're really being nice.

KELLY: It's no big deal.

(TRACY hands KELLY the water bottle. Their hands touch. An awkward moment.)

TRACY: . . .

KELLY: Go back in and finish your paper.

TRACY: No! God, no. I'm going to crawl into a sewer somewhere and die.

KELLY: No. Read the rest of your report to me now. Focus. These are the only words that need to come out of your mouth. Okay?

TRACY: Okay.

(TRACY gathers up pages from her paper, which are scattered around her. She reorders them and finds the last paragraph.)

TRACY: *(CONT.)* The poem ends with Keats' knight-in-arms awaking from his dream:

I saw their starved lips in the gloam,
With horrid warning gaped wide,
And I awoke and found me here,
On the cold hill's side.
And this is why I sojourn here
Alone and palely loitering,
Though the sedge is withered from the lake,
And no birds sing.

The dream of a world without mercy, without pity, has left the poor knight alone and pale. He is lingering on the cold hill's side in reverberant shock from his brush with cruelty. It's an inhospitable place he has chosen to grieve for his loss of hope. The sedge, a form of flowering grass, has withered and no birds sing. But there is an unstated optimism to the poem. If the lonely, pale, withered, and silent mood Keats creates is brought about by the lack of pity and mercy in the world, there is an implied opposite. If only someone brought mercy and pity to the world, then it might blossom forth. And the birds would sing again. It would be a shared communion of souls, vibrant, fertile, and alive with song. A message that is as powerful today, and probably more powerful today, than when he wrote it.

KELLY: That's wonderful.

(TRACY starts panic breathing again. She gets it under control).

TRACY: Your name is Kelly, right?

KELLY: Right.

TRACY: I'm—

KELLY: You're Tracy.

TRACY: Yeah. . . . Do you want to get something to eat? After class. Maybe coffee? Whatever.

KELLY: Oh. Yeah. Sure.

TRACY: Good.

KELLY: Okay.

TRACY: Thanks.

KELLY: My pleasure.

(KELLY takes the water bottle back out of her bag and hands it to TRACY. This time they are careful not to touch.

KELLY exits.

TRACY pants and has another small panic attack. She forces herself to calm down and breathe. She takes a long drink. She breathes deeply a moment.)

TRACY:
I met a lady in the meads,
Full beautiful - a faery's child,
Her hair was long, her foot was light,
And her eyes were wild.

3. AND ON THY CHEEKS A FADING ROSE

KELLY's apartment. Continuous from scene one.

KELLY: That's mine. It was hanging over my bed. It was just a mistake that it was sent to you.

ELIZABETH: Oh. I see.

KELLY: We were friends. We were best friends. That's all.

ELIZABETH: You said you had her last journal.

KELLY: . . .

ELIZABETH: . . .

KELLY: Yeah.

ELIZABETH: The one I have-- the one that this Tiffany sent me-- stops a few months before she met you. So the journal you have must be from the time she met you to just before she died.

KELLY: Right.

ELIZABETH: Could you get it?

KELLY: *(makes a small noise)* . . . .

ELIZABETH: . . .

KELLY: It's . . . . It's private.

ELIZABETH: I see.

KELLY: Please. . . .

ELIZABETH: I was having a phone conversation with her once. A few months before she died. Just before Valentine's Day. I said something like, "Hey, Kiddo. Why don't we surprise Daddy by flying you out for a weekend? You can be his Valentine." We both knew that I was the one who wanted her. Daddy would peck her on the cheek, grunt, fart a little less because she was home, and stay glued to college basketball on ESPN. . . . But I would come alive again. Getting her room ready. Cooking for her. Getting my hair and nails done. You have to try and look nice with a young daughter to compete with-- naturally! . . . Christ . . . My looks went down the toilet when she died. . . . She said she couldn't get away. She had to study. And I heard giggling. But not from her. From someone else in the room. A female voice. But so close to the phone. Like someone had their mouth very near hers. And Tracy said, "shush." Softly. Like she was talking to a child or a small animal. Just "shush." Very tender. And I guess I knew. But I didn't say anything. Because I hoped I was wrong. Instead, I told a long story about the neighbor's cat, Mrs. Fuzzface. How one day Mrs. Fuzzface had been sleeping on the top of our van. And I drove off with her still up there, not realizing. And a truck driver on the freeway started honking at me and pointing. And I pulled over and there was Mrs. Fuzzface staring down at me. Scared me to death. But not her. She was sort of exhilarated, as near as I could tell, from the expression on her little feline face. Exhilarated at getting away with such a stunt. And Tracy laughed. But not the precious laugh she usually had for Mrs. Fuzzface. The laugh that reminded me of her first baby laughs. No. A grown-up laugh. Deeper. Longer. Throaty. Delighted with herself. And I knew. So I said goodbye, and I hung up.

KELLY: She said you wouldn't understand.

ELIZABETH: Did she?

KELLY: She said you voted to support some state initiative. Marriage means a man and a woman. You're republican. You wanted grandchildren, and she was your only child.

ELIZABETH: I see.

KELLY: She loved you so much. She wanted you to be proud of her.

ELIZABETH: I was.

KELLY: Right.

ELIZABETH: Right.

(ELIZABETH crosses to look at a picture of Rachel Corrie on KELLY's wall. Rachel is burning the American flag in front of young Palestinian children.)

KELLY: . . .

ELIZABETH: . . .

KELLY: She really loved you.

ELIZABETH: You know, I don't think I've ever been in a lesbian apartment before.

KELLY: The apartment's asexual. I'm the lesbian.

ELIZABETH: I'm sorry. Was that an insulting remark? I'm trying to relearn tact. I lost all capacity for tact when my daughter's mutilated body was returned to me in a sealed box and I couldn't even touch her dead skin. So I don't know if I'm offending you. All my little sensory organs, the ones that are supposed to tingle with warning if I am giving someone *offense*, were seared away, melted from my body, and fused into the dirt at *All Saint's Cemetery*. I think that's where I left them. At her grave. So tact is like a sixth sense of the body that I'm cut off from now. You'll have to lead me around any issues you are sensitive about as if I were a blind woman.

KELLY: . . .

ELIZABETH: I don't know what I expected in a *lesbian's* apartment. I guess more flags like the one I got in the mail. Hanging in the doorways, used as curtains, serving as tablecloths. Perhaps artwork featuring large pink triangles. Certainly framed adoring photos of Ellen Degeneres. Some of those strap on dildos you see people wear on HBO's *Real Sex*, perhaps hung casually from all the doorknobs.

KELLY: Well, I haven't been into decorating lately. I'm sure I'll get around to it.

ELIZABETH: Hmmm. You seem to have found time to thumbtack flag-burning zealots to the wall. Who is this?

KELLY: Rachel Corrie.

ELIZABETH: I thought so. Some newspaper reporter called me. Just after Tracy's body was flown home. I

37

don't know why I picked up the phone. We mostly kept it unplugged from the wall then. She suggested I contact Rachel Corrie's mother and start a *support group*. I laughed until I was almost sick. And then I dropped the phone into the garbage disposal. Bill pulled it out later. Shook his head over it. . . . Who are these other people? Who is this?

KELLY: Lech Walesa.

ELIZABETH: The Pole. From the 80s.

KELLY: The Polish labor organizer. From the Solidarity movement—

ELIZABETH: And this?

KELLY: Cesar Chavez. He was a Mexican labor leader and organizer—

ELIZABETH: I know who he was. Thank you. Who's the Indian fellow?

KELLY: That's Babaji. He's a guru. He transcended his mortal state and became one with the divine life force. But he refused to leave the mortal plane and stays with us to help seekers of enlightenment.

ELIZABETH: You're kind of a nut, aren't you?

KELLY: . . .

ELIZABETH: You really seem to identify with the wrong sort of people. That's all I'm saying.

KELLY: I identify with people who try to make a differ-
ence.

ELIZABETH: No. You identify with people that mobs
of violent peasants want to tear limb from limb. I
don't know about Bab-whatsit, Mr.-Too-Good-For-
the-Planet, but these others—

KELLY: Lech Walesa is a former president of Poland.
He won the Nobel Prize. No one tore him limb from
limb. He's alive-

ELIZABETH: People wanted to kill him.

KELLY: People wanted to kill Gandhi.

ELIZABETH: Exactly. I wouldn't consider him a role
model, either.

KELLY: You think Gandhi is not a role model?

ELIZABETH: Of course not.

KELLY: He stood up for an entire nation when no one
else had the guts to. He changed the world.

ELIZABETH: He painted a big target on himself.

KELLY: He's an icon.

ELIZABETH: He put his family in jeopardy. It's a miracle he wasn't tortured to death like my daughter.

KELLY: . . .

ELIZABETH: . . .

KELLY: So, the world you want to live in is a world where nobody stands up for freedom? Where we all just accept persecution to be safe? I can't accept that. Somebody has to step out of the crowd and say, "this is unacceptable." And you don't have to put yourself at risk to do it; you don't have to be violent. You can just send letters. You can just speak up at rotary club meetings, at city councils, at the PTA. You can make phone calls. Send money anonymously. But you can't just do *nothing*. There is so much injustice out there. So many wrong things happening in this city, this country, this world. And if you see the problem, you are morally obligated to help solve it. It becomes *your* problem. Because there are millions of people who don't even see what's happening. Each of the people on this wall are like torchbearers leading us to a better place—

ELIZABETH: You're very good.

KELLY: What?

ELIZABETH: I bet before Colombia you were unstoppable. I bet the passion just poured out of you. It's a little muted now. But still very compelling.

KELLY: I am passionate. About this.

ELIZABETH: Oh, I know you are.

KELLY: Gandhi was a great leader—

ELIZABETH: Oh, don't get worked up. I don't care about Gandhi. I just wanted to see it.

KELLY: See what?

ELIZABETH: What Tracy died for.

KELLY: . . . .

ELIZABETH: . . .

KELLY: You . . blame . . . me?

ELIZABETH: . . .

KELLY: . . .

ELIZABETH: Of course I blame you. . . . My daughter was a literature major when she met you. She was reading Fanny Burney and discovering that feminist novels pre-date Jane Austen. It was a beautiful moment in her life. Her cheeks were always the shade of red you see on china dolls. She looked good in Abercrombie & Fitch, like a model. She was going to a student-led bible study. She voted republican like her father and me. She had a crush on a boy who worked as a sports' editor on the college newspaper. What the hell happened to that boy? Where did he go? Jesus, did he just disappear? Sometimes I spend whole days fantasizing about that boy. I don't remember his name. Philip? Peter? Jonathan? I fantasize that he got her pregnant. That he got her hooked on drugs. That he beat her. That she became so crazy about him she dropped out of school. I come up with every bad situation I can think of that two young kids could get into. And in the fantasy I fly down to California and save her. Abort the unwanted brat, lock her ass in rehab, set him up with anger management classes, or hire someone from *Soldier of Fortune* magazine to break his kneecaps. I want that boy for her. Because I can think of a thousand ways the little punk might have ruined her life. But he wouldn't have *ended it*! He wouldn't have taken her where you took her. Not that boy. Not whatshisname.

KELLY: . . .

ELIZABETH: . . .

KELLY: His name was Joshua. He was gay. She went to a party at his apartment, and he introduced her to his lover. That's how she found out.

ELIZABETH: Oh. . . . Terrific. Another one. What is this UCI? University of Closeted Individuals? Were there no heterosexual students for her to mix with? Why isn't this in the promotional literature? "Send your child to our lovely campus, so we can expand her mind in directions you don't want it expanded?"

KELLY: . . .

ELIZABETH: . . .

KELLY: I blame myself, too. Every day.

ELIZABETH: . . .

KELLY: And I think about killing myself. I think about it a lot. I'm trying to think of a way to do it. I'm such a baby. Since getting shot, I can't stand the thought of pain. You'd think it would toughen me up. Give me some sort of defense. I was, you know, lying there for something like twelve hours in pain. The bullet just grazed me, but the fall shattered the leg bones. And I couldn't think of anything but the pain. And Tracy. I worried about her and I cried with pain. That's all I did for twelve hours. Until the U'wa found me. And since then, if someone even describes a paper cut to me, I get this reflexive, sympathetic, paralyzing wave of agony. Sometimes I'll turn on the TV and there'll be a Western on. And some Apache warrior will put an arrow through the hero's side, and I'll just curl up into this whimpering, trembling ball on the couch and not be able to move. So, I want to find a way that doesn't hurt. Stupid. I know the pain wouldn't last more than a minute if I got a gun. Less than a second. But I think about those twelve hours and there's just this little crying child inside me. . . . I'm seeing this psychiatrist. My mom set it up. Doesn't help. . . . . And I understand what you feel. About me. About blaming me. I would feel the same. And I'm even grateful for it. If you were one of those women you see on talk shows who go around forgiving the serial child molester who raped and killed their second grader, I wouldn't know what to do. I really think I would probably lose respect for you. I think this way, we're better off. We're on the same page. I understand you.

ELIZABETH: . . .

KELLY: . . .

ELIZABETH: Well. . . if I were your mom, I do the same. The psychiatrist doesn't do you any good?

KELLY: No.

ELIZABETH: When I was hospitalized, I hated the psychiatrists. Sanctimonious, puffed-up, little pill-pushers. Mine did nothing but medicate me. As if all I needed as a good sleep. I guess they thought if I could hibernate like a black bear, or sleep a hundred years like Briar Rose, the wounds would all heal of their own accord.

KELLY: I wouldn't want the wounds to heal fully.

ELIZABETH: That's true isn't it? You don't want them too. You'd rather walk around every day until the end of time with this disfiguring mass of bloody scars covering your face than have the tiniest wound heal.

KELLY: If the wounds heal it means you're forgetting her.

ELIZABETH: Any lessening of your agony means your attachment to her is weakening.

KELLY: It means you love her less.

ELIZABETH: It's disrespectful to her memory to get over this. I tell my husband that over and over and over again. But he doesn't get it. He says, "When are things going to get back to normal?" I say, "Never." I don't want normal. I want abnormal. I want to cut gouges out of my cheeks, blind myself in one eye, and slit my nostrils open like a pig. So that when I walk down the street, mothers pull their children out of my path and grown men weep. And everyone I see says, "Oh my god, what happened to her? She has suffered something terrible, something disfiguring, something cruel and punishing, something that must be respected, something that it tortures our souls to witness!" That's what I want. That's my normal.

KELLY: . . .

ELIZABETH: . . .

KELLY: Yeah. I get that.

ELIZABETH: You do . . . . You do get it.

KELLY: . . .

ELIZABETH: . . .

KELLY: I don't think I've ever had a really deep conversation with a Republican before.

ELIZABETH: I'm seeing my first lesbian apartment, and you're having tea with the devil, huh?

KELLY: I guess you hurt the same as us.

ELIZABETH: I don't think so. I don't hurt for the damned U'wa Indians. If I had a time machine I would go back and help Cortez infect the entire tribe with small pox. I hurt for my daughter. The rest of the world can sort itself out.

KELLY: You don't want to help people?

ELIZABETH: I want to protect what's mine first and help others second.

KELLY: Tracy wanted to help people.

ELIZABETH: Tracy was 22 years old.

KELLY: She was filled with love.

ELIZABETH: Perverse love.

KELLY: You think it was a phase she would have grown out of?

ELIZABETH: Activism?

KELLY: Lesbianism.

ELIZABETH: Oh. That.

KELLY: You think she would have grown out of loving me?

ELIZABETH: I hope she would have.

KELLY: . . .

ELIZABETH: I'm sorry. But I do hope she would have.

KELLY: Okay.

ELIZABETH: . . .

KELLY: I'll get her things now. You can take them.

ELIZABETH: When I was in grad school, I read a great deal of literary criticism. And I read something in a book by Gaston Bachelard that I have never forgotten. It was a book on poetic reverie, and in the first chapter he gave his definition of love. "Love is the intersection," he said, "of two poetries." Two people are stumbling around in the world. And each exists in his or her own personal bubble of poetic pain and lyrical dreams. And then one day the two people collide and share some of their interior madness with one another. And if the poetries overlap, if they build and resonate together, if they cradle and reinforce one another, we call it *love*.... But our personal poetry is mad. Look at the poetry you and I are filled with. It's the stuff of nightmares. And it's all like that. Inside every human, there's a locked cabinet of vicious demons. And they decide who we love. The demons.

KELLY: . . .

ELIZABETH: She might have changed someday. Learned a different poetry. I hope she would have.

KELLY: . . .

(KELLY exits to the bedroom.)

4. AND HONEY WILD, AND MANNA-DEW

TRACY sits on a beanbag in a dorm suite.

TRACY: And she had around ten romance novels in her office, sitting on her desk. All I could think about was how you and I were making fun of her. After she was reading one during the pop quiz. I almost laughed out loud.

KELLY: *(O.S.)* You should have.

TRACY: I mean, she had ten of them on her desk. During my conference time. It was like she had a big stack of porn sitting there. The one on the top of the stack was called *The Secret Pearl*. It had this pink cover that made me think of vaginas. And *The Secret Pearl* just made me think about clitorises. It was really uncomfortable.

KELLY: *(O.S.)* What did she say about your presentation?

TRACY: She liked it. I got a lecture, of course, on improving my public speaking.

(KELLY enters, from the kitchen with a bottle of uncorked wine and two plastic cups.)

KELLY: She *lectured* you?

TRACY: Well, maybe gentler than lectured. She was trying to be motherly. Although she doesn't have children. You can sort of tell that she just has romance novels and a tribe of cats. Which makes me feel bad about making fun of her, because really, life is already doing that. But she can be so annoying. She didn't go on about it. Just asked if I was feeling better. She didn't make it an issue.

KELLY: I told you it wasn't a big deal.

TRACY: And then she told me I got the highest grade in class.

KELLY: I knew you would! I knew it! You were brilliant.

TRACY: But I should participate more. Because I have a lot to offer, and I can't offer it if I don't learn to speak up. Let my voice be heard.

KELLY: That's exactly what I said. Look, I got it open.

TRACY: Did you have to cut it out with a knife?

KELLY: One of my roommates had a corkscrew. It was at the back of a drawer.

TRACY: You're lucky to be in a suite. I don't have a kitchen. I have to go down a floor to microwave popcorn.

KELLY: That sucks.

TRACY: Yeah.

KELLY: You know, one of my roommates is moving out over winter break.

TRACY: Which one?

KELLY: Chloe. She's going to Italy.

TRACY: Lucky.

KELLY: We could put in the paperwork. You could transfer in.

TRACY: Really?

KELLY: Sure. If you want.

TRACY: It would be better than the single I have.

KELLY: Why do you have a single?

TRACY: My last roommate was crazy. She brought guys over in the middle of the night. Like three guys at a time. I had to either pretend to be asleep or go sit in the shower room all night. Gross.

KELLY: Who was that?

TRACY: Lizette—

KELLY: Ohhh! I know who she is. She was your *room-mate*?

TRACY: Yeah. Everyone knows who she is. She's famous. I just decided to get a single after that.

KELLY: Well, if you want a kitchen, and to be part of a suite . . .

TRACY: When do you leave? For Colombia?

KELLY: I'm taking Spring Break and then a week after that.

TRACY: So you have some time. To get ready.

KELLY: Yeah. I'm pretty much ready, though.

TRACY: So, the mountain that the petroleum company is drilling on is sacred to that Indian tribe?

KELLY: The U'was. They call themselves "the thinking people." Because they're pacifists. The mountain they want to save is called Mother Earth. Their religion tells them that the oil is the blood of Mother Earth. So it can't be removed without killing her and killing their whole belief system.

TRACY: And the government in Colombia won't help them?

KELLY: Are you serious? No. The government is on Occidental Petroleum's side. See the country is in the middle of a civil war. There are these rebel groups, the FARC and ELN, who control almost half of the country. And they control the area around the U'wa sacred sites. So the government *wants* the petroleum company to drill on the land, because they bring security personnel and American money to help fight the rebels and control the region.

TRACY: Oh.

KELLY: So the rebels are actually the ones resisting the drilling. Bombing pipelines and destroying machinery. But the U'wa's don't support that. Because they're pacifists. They want to resist without violence. And they desperately need help.

TRACY: How did you learn about them?

KELLY: I was president of the Amnesty International chapter at my high school in Sausalito, and a speaker came and talked to us about them.

TRACY: I really admire you for getting involved like that. It's really brave.

KELLY: It's too important not to get involved. This tribe's whole religion is at stake. And not just that. It's bigger than that.

TRACY: Well, it sets a precedent, doesn't it? That small voices won't be heard. That different ideas about religion and the way the world works are not important. That capitalism is more important than faith and community.

KELLY: Yes. All that. And because of who the U'wa are and how they define themselves. I mean, they speak *U'wajka*, their native language. They haven't adopted Spanish. They practice their traditional religion, worshipping *Yagshowa*, their god. They've resisted any efforts at colonization since the seventeenth century. But resisted without violence. When the Spanish *conquistadores* came to Colombia and tried to enslave the U'wa, the chieftain of the largest clan, took all his people to the tops of these huge, beautiful cliffs I've seen in photographs. They call them "the Cliffs of Glory." And the chieftain told them that the U'wa would never live as slaves, and they would also never raise their hands in violence toward other humans. So they sealed all their children in clay pots and threw them over the cliff's edge. And the adults all held hands and walked backwards off the cliff.

KELLY *(CONT.)*: And they have vowed to do this again. If the blood of the Mother Earth is stolen from their sacred lands, the entire tribe will once again throw themselves off the Cliffs of Glory.

TRACY: Oh, my god.

KELLY: Ignoring this is not an option.

TRACY: What are you going to do to help them? When you get there?

KELLY: We're going to see what they need. We're going to film everything for a documentary. A film crew was coming, but they backed out. So it's just me and Ben, who leads the Amnesty International group at UC Davis. But I have a digital camera.

TRACY: So, it's just the two of you?

KELLY: Yeah. But that's probably better. It'll be easier for us to travel around. And there won't be equipment to haul.

TRACY: Do you worry at all that something might happen?

KELLY: A little.

TRACY: But you're going anyway.

KELLY: I'm going anyway.

TRACY: It's good you don't have a boyfriend then. He'd worry about you while you're gone.

KELLY: I don't have anyone now. But I'm not leaving until spring break. There's room for developments in that area.

TRACY: . . .

KELLY: . . .

TRACY: We should drink this.

KELLY: We should.

(KELLY pours wine into the cups.)

TRACY: What are we celebrating?

KELLY: You getting the highest grade in the class. Professor McDonaugh tried to distract you by waving that wild thatch of permed gorilla hair in your face to confuse and disturb you. To make you think, "No wonder you sleep naked with your fifteen rescued cats, you sad old bag." But you resisted all of that! You stayed focused and you took top honors! Cheers!

(They drink.)

TRACY: I did okay.

KELLY: You were amazing. I got a C, you know. I'm not in your league. Nowhere close.

TRACY: That's not true! Grades don't mean anything. You're such a better person than I am. When I ran out of class hyperventilating, I really think you-- . . . I don't know.

KELLY: What?

TRACY: I think you saved my life or something.

KELLY: Nobody dies of a panic attack.

TRACY: No. I know. But, it wasn't just that. I'm a sophomore here. And my whole first year, I spent cowering in a shower stall because my roommate was gang-banging entire frat houses in our room. And I spent most of that time crying. Not because of Lizette, because she probably has every disease known to man, and she'll totally get hers. And who really cares? But I just hate myself for not being able to say anything. I never even had it out with her, you know? I never even said stop it, this hurts me. Sometimes I'd be too scared to go sit in the shower stall, and I'd just lie there and listen. Listen to her and whoever she brought home. And, I've never . . . you know. I just never did, and this is the first time I'm hearing some of this stuff. And it's like she's . . . ruining something for me. Because I don't like it, and it's really loud, and it just makes me a little sick. And I just die a little inside, you know? Sometimes it's just disgusting, and sometimes I'm a little jealous. And I didn't even switch rooms over Christmas break, because I was worried about hurting her feelings. I was worried about hurting *her* feelings. Isn't that a joke? . . .I'm not strong like you. You take care of yourself so well, you have enough left over to go and protect whole South American tribes from throwing themselves off cliffs. You're planning to stop a self-inflicted geno-cide with just a camcorder and a guy from UC Davis. And I can see you doing it. Putting your own body between those people and the cliffs and making them listen to you. I couldn't even tell my ex-roommate to go screw somewhere else. I don't have that kind of voice. I don't have a voice that can fight, that can plead, that can say something strongly if opposed, that can argue, or that can even disagree. It's like a note I just can't hit. I try and my voice breaks. . . .

(TRACY starts to hyperventilate. KELLY grabs her hands.)

KELLY: Breathe. Just-- It's okay. Breathe.

(TRACY and KELLY take a couple deep breaths together. Then TRACY lets go of KELLY's hands.)

TRACY: Sorry. I'm sorry. I wasn't going to go back into class after my panic attack. I was going to leave my purse and everything and just go hide in the toilet. Pull my legs up onto the toilet bowl and hope nobody came looking for me. Because I'm not strong. I'm not strong at all. But you came after me, and we talked. And I just borrowed your strength. I just reached out and borrowed it. I think I pretended I was you. I went back in the room. And you smiled at me and winked. And I had the strength. It probably didn't mean much to you, because I bet you're kind to people and do nice things for them everyday. But people haven't been kind to me like that. And I can live off kindness like that a long time. And I did Keats justice. For once I didn't disappoint him. I did his beautiful poem, that piece of poetry I love, some justice.

I met a lady in the meads,
Full beautiful - a faery's child,
Her hair was long, her foot was light,
And her eyes were wild.
I made a garland for her head,

And bracelets too, and fragrant zone;
She looked at me as she did love,
And made sweet moan.

(KELLY kisses her, then breaks away.)

KELLY: I'm sorry.

TRACY: No.

KELLY: I'm so sorry.

TRACY: No. It's okay.

KELLY: It's not. It's not okay. It isn't. You were telling me something very real and I jumped on you afterward. I just jumped on you. And that's gross.

TRACY: It's not.

KELLY: Look. I'm sorry. When I said I didn't have a boyfriend . . .

TRACY: Yes?

KELLY: I just sort of went with that. Because we were getting to be friends and I like you and I want you to like me.

TRACY: You're a lesbian?

KELLY: Yes. And I didn't say it, because I thought you might think I'm just friends with you because I want to hit on you or something. Because you're pretty. That would be sick. I just want to know you and be with you. Be friends.

TRACY: Okay.

KELLY: Because you get upset with yourself a lot, and I know what that's like. And I don't want you to feel that way. To be down on yourself. That's just a miserable way to feel.

TRACY: Okay. Thanks.

KELLY: And I wasn't hitting on you. And I'm really babbling now. Jesus.

TRACY: No, I'm not-- . . . I'm not feeling weird or anything.

KELLY: Good. Let's stop talking about it then. I feel like a creep. And I'm not like that. We were talking about something real. And you were telling me something important. Those things you said-- . . .they were like a gift to me. And I should have respected—

(TRACY kisses her back.)

KELLY: Wow. Okay. Wow. . . Um. . . Do you really want . . . Because maybe you're just curious, but not really interested in—

TRACY: I'm interested.

KELLY: Right. Look, what you said about not being strong. I think you're wrong. I think you're very strong. But if you're just doing this because you think it will make me happy. Don't think about making me happy. Be very selfish about this. Because if you aren't being very selfish about what you want, then what you're doing is sort of selfish. You know? Because it means everything to me. And if it doesn't mean that much to you, I'm the one who is going to end up crying.

TRACY: You'll never cry over me. I'll never break your heart like that. I promise.

(TRACY takes off her clothes. KELLY looks at her a moment. She removes her own clothes. They kiss and fall to the floor, touching one another.)

5. AND THERE I SHUT HER WILD WILD EYES

The tea kettle screams in KELLY's apartment. The lights come up on ELIZABETH who is startled for a moment. She gets up and goes to stand over the kettle, looking at it as if it were a sinister and unfamiliar object.

After a moment, in which ELIZABETH fumbles uselessly around the kitchen, cursing the kettle and looking for a pot holder, KELLY enters with a box. She sets the box on the floor by the couch and goes to the tea kettle.

ELIZABETH: I was going to take the thing off the burner, but I couldn't figure out what to do with it after that. I only know how to make tea in bags. French press sounds like some strange venereal disease to me.

KELLY: I got it.

(KELLY pours the water into her french press)

ELIZABETH: Thanks.

(KELLY unwraps some flax crackers and puts them on a plate.)

ELIZABETH: *(CONT.)* What are those?

KELLY: They're flax crackers.

ELIZABETH: What's a flax cracker?

KELLY: They're crackers that have been dehydrated instead of baked. Not heated past 120 degrees. So they retain all of their digestive enzymes. They're made with flax and vegetable juices. They're part of my diet.

ELIZABETH: What diet?

KELLY: Well, it's a lifestyle choice really. I shouldn't use the word diet. It isn't temporary. . . . I only eat raw foods. Nothing cooked. And no animal products.

ELIZABETH: So, you only eat raw, what? Fruits and vegetables?

KELLY: Yes.

ELIZABETH: What about bread? No bread?

KELLY: It's cooked.

ELIZABETH: Nothing but raw fruits and vegetables?

KELLY: And nuts. Seeds. Things like that.

ELIZABETH: So mostly, what? Salads.

KELLY: Yeah. And I have recipe books.

(KELLY hands ELIZABETH a recipe book. ELIZABETH leafs through it. KELLY pours them some tea.)

ELIZABETH: Well. I guess you wouldn't call it a cook-book, would you? Sprouted quinoa salad with radishes and curry sauce. Sounds healthy. You don't look like you need to lose any weight.

KELLY: It's not just for weight loss. It's cleansing. It's very healthy. It's spiritually sustainable in a way that eating meat really isn't.

ELIZABETH: How long are you going to eat this way?

KELLY: The rest of my life. It gives me comfort.

ELIZABETH: It sounds like punishment. It sounds like you're sending yourself to bed without supper. For the rest of your life. How long have been doing it?

KELLY: Almost three years.

ELIZABETH: So right after—

KELLY: Yeah. Right after.

(ELIZABETH tries a flax cracker.)

ELIZABETH: Interesting. I stopped eating for about four months. Right after. But I like your approach better. It's almost poetic. Like you're keeping a vigil for her. A raw food vigil.

(KELLY eats a flax cracker.)

KELLY: I try not to eat anything that has died so that I can eat it. I'll stick to things like fruit and seeds and nuts for months at a time. Because it doesn't kill the plant to harvest those. I just can't stand the thought of anything else dying for me.

ELIZABETH: It must keep you busy. Planning and making these strange meals. You probably have to shop more frequently than you would otherwise, to get food that's fresh.

KELLY: Yes.

ELIZABETH: And all that takes time off the clock and distracts you. I used to hate crap that ate time that way. I was the worst housekeeper. Always had piles of dishes in the sink. We ate fast food because I refused to spend time in the kitchen. Now I can just lose myself for hours doing that sort of thing. And I'm grateful for it.

KELLY: I'm grateful for indifferent people now. It used to really bother me, people who don't respond to other people's pain. It used to be a big issue for me. I thought we should all feel deeply and should all be available to one another all the time. But now, I might be standing in the supermarket and just start crying. And the people I hate are the ones who acknowledge it. Try to help when there's just no way they can help. I love the people who look right through me and just keep shopping. I'm deeply grateful for them.

ELIZABETH: I'm grateful for the fact that I have never forgotten she's gone. Not for a second. Not waking, not sleeping, not in between waking and sleeping, not while daydreaming, not in a moment of lulled distraction. Never. I have always remembered. Some poor people, they go to sleep and when they wake up they forget for a split second. Expect to see their daughter come skipping into the room, right as rain. And they relive the whole experience of realizing she's gone in a split second. Or they think they see her in a crowd and forget for a moment. Or they're at the mall looking at clothes and think, "oh, this would look good on my daughter," before they remember she's gone. Their mind betrays them like that. Mine never has and I'm grateful.

KELLY: You're lucky. I see her everywhere. And I forget in my dreams.

ELIZABETH: She's dead in my dreams. She's always dead. . . . I wouldn't mind seeing her living once or twice in my dreams.

KELLY: Yeah. It can be nice.

(They drink their tea.)

ELIZABETH: So what's in the box?

KELLY: I'll get it.

(KELLY starts to get up.)

ELIZABETH: Don't get it. I don't want you to get it. I want you to tell me what's in it. So I'm not surprised.

KELLY: . . .

ELIZABETH: . . .

KELLY: Her backpack. The one she was carrying. In the backpack: two pairs of jeans; one of those colorful South American pullovers we bought for cheap in Buenaventura; a red T-shirt; a heather blue T-shirt; a sports bra; two pairs of panties; some receipts from food we bought at the airport; her cellphone; some tampons; a notebook she was taking notes in for an article she wanted to write for the campus newspaper; a BIC four color pen; her hairbrush; her passport; her deodorant; a water bottle; a Luna bar; her skin cream; a tube of lip gloss; sunglasses; her dorm room keys; her journal; she kept her necklace with the little gold and diamond heart in a side pocket of the backpack, so no one would see it on her and steal it; her wallet. In the wallet: fifteen American dollars and seventy-four cents; a ticket stub from a Harry Potter movie we saw together; her credit card, the one you cosigned for; a picture of the cat she had in high school, Baxter; a picture of her dad, Bill; a picture of the two of us. Then I have the clothes they cut off her when they raped us. A pair of khaki cargo pants. Pink panties with white flowers. A grey sports bra. A light blue, button front cotton shirt with dark blue flowers and little green leaves. It doesn't have any buttons anymore. They cut them off. Her socks. Her hiking boots. A bandana that she wore in her hair. They gagged her with it and she cried into it. There are some grass stains. And there are dirt stains. And there is some blood on the clothes. That's everything the U'wa could find. That's everything they brought me.

ELIZABETH: . . .

KELLY: . . .

ELIZABETH: Bring me the backpack.

(KELLY goes to the box and gets the backpack. She hands it to ELIZABETH. ELIZABETH puts the backpack on the counter in front of her. She goes into her own bag and finds a pair of reading glasses. She puts on the glasses and unzips the backpack.

KELLY goes and sits in a canvas chair. She takes the blue button-front shirt from the box and looks at it. ELIZABETH unzips the backpack and takes out the hairbrush. She touches the hair caught in the bristles.)

ELIZABETH: Do you have a pair of scissors?

(KELLY puts down the shirt and goes to the desk. She finds scissors and brings them to ELIZABETH.)

ELIZABETH: *(CONT.)* I want to keep her hairbrush.

KELLY: Okay.

ELIZABETH: I'll leave you . . . I'll leave you half of the hair.

KELLY: . . .

(ELIZABETH carefully lifts half of the hair from the brush and cuts it free. She tucks the rest of the hair back into the bristles. She hands KELLY her half of the hair.)

KELLY: *(CONT.)* Thank you.

(ELIZABETH sets the hairbrush aside and pulls out the sunglasses.)

ELIZABETH: You can have these. I never saw her wear them.

(She sets the sunglasses on the opposite side of the counter from the hairbrush. The sunglasses are KELLY's pile and the hairbrush is ELIZABETH's pile. She reaches in and pulls out the deodorant. She puts that in her pile. She pulls out the water bottle. That goes in KELLY's pile. KELLY watches ELIZABETH pull out the passport. That goes in ELIZABETH's pile. She pulls out the skin cream, that goes in KELLY's pile. She pulls out the cellphone. It goes in ELIZABETH's pile. The South American pullover goes in KELLY's pile. The red and heather blue T-shirts are next, they go in ELIZABETH's pile.)

KELLY: *(makes a small noise)* . . .

ELIZABETH: What?

(KELLY takes the skin cream from her pile and puts it be-tween the two piles. She points at the heather blue T-shirt. ELIZABETH moves the skin cream into her own pile and puts the T-shirt in KELLY's pile. KELLY takes the T-shirt and smells it. She carries it to the couch. She hugs it. She holds it to her mouth.

ELIZABETH puts one pair of jeans in her pile and one pair of jeans in KELLY's. The sports bra goes in KELLY's pile. One tampon goes in each pile. One pair of panties in each pile.

KELLY puts the T-shirt on. She takes the bandana out of the box and puts it on the arm of the couch. She puts her half of the hair on top of it. She puts the blue button-front below the bandana, as if TRACY were lying stretched out on the couch. The gray sports bra goes underneath the shirt. Then the cargo pants are laid out. The pink panties are placed gently inside the pants. She puts the socks in the boots and sets them at the ankles of the pants. She steps back to look at the clothes. There are grass, dirt, and blood stains. She touches each of the stains.

ELIZABETH is still sorting. The notebook goes in KELLY's pile and the journal goes in ELIZABETH's. She stops and thinks about that for a moment. She opens the notebook and reads a page. She puts that down. She opens the journal and reads a page. She puts that down much more quickly. She changes her mind and puts the notebook on her pile and the journal on KELLY's pile. She puts the BIC pen in her pile. She puts the Luna bar in KELLY's pile. She stops and thinks about that and peers closely at the wrapper. She holds the bar up.)

67

ELIZABETH: You can't eat this, right? It's cooked.

KELLY: Right.

ELIZABETH: Well, I'm not going to eat it either. But I'm trying to be fair.

(ELIZABETH puts the Luna bar on her own pile.)

KELLY: . . .

(ELIZABETH puts the receipts in KELLY's pile. The lip gloss also goes in KELLY's pile. The dorm room keys go in ELIZABETH's pile. She finds the necklace in a side pocket of the backpack. She removes the gold heart from the chain. The chain goes in KELLY's pile. The gold heart goes in ELIZABETH's pile. She takes out the wallet. She opens the wallet and removes the Harry Potter ticket stub, and the picture of KELLY and TRACY- these things go into KELLY's pile. The rest of the wallet goes into ELIZABETH's pile. ELIZABETH puts her pile into the backpack and zips it shut.)

ELIZABETH: Do you have some plastic bags I could wrap this in? I don't want to get it wet.

KELLY: Sure.

(KELLY goes into the kitchen to find the bags. ELIZABETH turns and sees what KELLY has done to the clothes.)

ELIZABETH: . . . .

(KELLY gets a handful of plastic Whole Foods bags. She holds them out to ELIZABETH.)

KELLY: Here.

ELIZABETH: . . .

KELLY: I'm out of garbage bags. I don't have anything bigger.

ELIZABETH: . . .

(ELIZABETH walks over the couch. She takes off her reading glasses and stands looking down at the clothes. KELLY starts wrapping the backpack in plastic bags. She sighs and stops.)

KELLY: Are you mad at me? . . . . Look, I don't know why I did it. Set the clothes out like that. Like she was lying there. . . . Sometimes I like to pretend. You said that you don't ever see her. In a crowd of people. And you're glad you don't. Because you'd get that thrill of hope and just have it crushed again. Well, I don't mind the crushing. I don't care if I feel the whole loss all over again every minute of the day, but I can't live without that brief, irrational spark of hope. Without seeing her in strangers' faces. Without thinking I hear her voice behind me in the supermarket line. These are the reasons I get out of bed in the morning. And so I'm sorry if I hurt you. And if you're mad.

ELIZABETH: . . .

KELLY: . . .

ELIZABETH: I'm not mad at you. Why would I be mad at you? I think it's . . . I think it's beautiful. It's just beautiful. There is her hair. There are her tears dried into that cloth. There is her shirt that they tore off her.

And ripped the buttons. Her stained bra beneath it. They must have had to pull it off over her head. It's the kind with no clasps on it. I didn't know that's what she was wearing. There are her pants. They cut these near to pieces.

That must be her blood. And there are her little socks. Did they even take off the socks, or was she wearing them? . . . And her boots. I bought those boots for her. . . . I think it's beautiful. . . . I really do. I never got to see her body. . . . They wouldn't let me. . . . They said I was too fragile. . . . But look at me. . . . I'm not fragile. I'm looking at her body right now. And it's beautiful. It's the most beautiful thing I've seen. Since . . I . . last . . saw . . her . . face.

Oh, sweet Fancy! let her loose;
Every thing is spoilt by use:
Where's the cheek that doth not fade,
Too much gaz'd at? Where's the maid
Whose lip mature is ever new?
Where's the eye, however blue,
Doth not weary? Where's the face
One would meet in every place?
Where's the voice, however soft,
One would hear so very oft?
At a touch sweet Pleasure melteth
Like to bubbles when rain pelteth.
Let, then, winged Fancy find
Thee a mistress to thy mind:
Dulcet-ey'd as Ceres' daughter,
Ere the God of Torment taught her
How to frown and how to chide;
With a waist and with a side
White as Hebe's, when her zone
Slipt its golden clasp, and down

Fell her kirtle to her feet,
While she held the goblet sweet
And Jove grew languid.--Break the mesh
Of the Fancy's silken leash;
Quickly break her prison-string
And such joys as these she'll bring.--
Let the winged Fancy roam,
Pleasure never is at home.

KELLY: . . .

ELIZABETH: . . .

KELLY: . . .

ELIZABETH: . . .

KELLY: . . .

ELIZABETH: You can keep the clothes.

KELLY: Thank you.

ELIZABETH: . . .

KELLY: . . .

ELIZABETH: Is that everything then?

KELLY: Yes. . . No. I have some photos on my computer. From Colombia. Buenaventura. Places we went
before it happened.

ELIZABETH: You took a camera?

KELLY: Yes.

ELIZABETH: . . .

KELLY: Do you want to see them? Do you want to see the photos?

ELIZABETH: You can email those to me. Right?

KELLY: Yes.

ELIZABETH: I'll give you my email address.

(ELIZABETH takes a pen from the desk and writes her email address on a notepad.)

KELLY: I'll email them tonight. They'll be waiting for you when you get home.

ELIZABETH: Thank you. Is that all, then?

KELLY: . . .

ELIZABETH: . . .

KELLY: I don't know. Do you . . . Don't you . . . *(sighs)* ... Don't you want to know . . . What happened?

ELIZABETH: How she died?

KELLY: Yes.

ELIZABETH: . . .

KELLY: Someone must have told you what happened, I know. But that someone wasn't me. And I'm the only one who was there.

ELIZABETH: Right.

KELLY: I was there.

ELIZABETH: . . .

KELLY: . . .

ELIZABETH: Can I have some water, please?

(KELLY gets her some water.)

KELLY: Do you want to know?

ELIZABETH: Yes. I do.

KELLY: We had been in the U'wa village for three days. Near the Cliffs of Glory. We had seen some rebel troops the day before. But it was no big deal. The villagers gave them food and water. We thought they were on our side. We had a common enemy in Occidental Petroleum. And we had their permission to be there. So they had armored cars and machine guns and rifles. But they didn't worry us. We thought we were safe. Ben was talking to the tribal leaders, the *werjayás,* the ancient wise men, back at the village. Tracy and I took the camera and went to the cliffs. We wanted to get footage of the cliffs for a documentary film we were making—

ELIZABETH: It was a video camera?

KELLY: *(quickly)* There isn't any footage of her. . . . Just stills.

ELIZABETH: Okay.

KELLY: And so we were alone on the Cliffs of Glory. The villagers had been following us around a lot. Touching our hair. Just wanted to be near us. We were feeling kind of crowded actually. But the cliff site is sacred. Because of the suicides. And they let us go up there alone. To experience it. The soldiers came from the south. See there are two rebel armies in Colombia. Sometimes they're allies, but it's a pretty cautious alliance. And we had permission from the ELN to be in the village. And we thought that they would have cleared it with the FARC. The other group of rebels. Right? Because they told us it was safe. But they didn't. And it wasn't safe. Of course it wasn't.

ELIZABETH: . . .

KELLY: . . .

ELIZABETH: How did they find you?

KELLY: The U'wa told them where to look. They didn't realize. They didn't know what the soldiers would do. They thought we were all on the same side. Working to save Mother Earth. They're pacifists. The FARC didn't see the value in having three stupid American kids working on their behalf. They thought we'd be more valuable as hostages. That they could get money from our families for guns and ammunition. To support the guerrilla campaigns against the government and Occidental.

ELIZABETH: Why didn't they keep you as hostages?

KELLY: *(makes a small noise)* . . .

ELIZABETH: . . .

KELLY: Because I fought.

ELIZABETH: What were you doing when they found you?

KELLY: We thought we were safe. We were in love. It was beautiful there. . .

ELIZABETH: . . .

KELLY: . . .

ELIZABETH: I see.

(ELIZABETH drinks her water. Then she puts her head in hands. She shakes softly.)

6. THEY CRIED - 'LA BELLE DAME SANS MERCI / HATH THEE IN THRALL!'

TRACY is standing on the Cliffs of Glory. She wears the outfit that is on the couch in KELLY's apartment. She breathes deeply and looks out over the cliff's edge.)

TRACY: Oh, Kel! Oh, God! It's beautiful! I've never seen anything so beautiful. Oh, God! When my mom sees something this beautiful she quotes Keats. But I don't have much memorized. Not like she does. She's like a walking encyclopedia. All I can think of is:

How beautiful, if sorrow had not made
Sorrow more beautiful than Beauty's self.

And that sucks. It's not happy. And I'm happy! Maybe Keats isn't the best choice for happy. Are you listening to me?

(KELLY enters. She is filming TRACY with a digital camcorder.)

KELLY: No. I'm watching you. Hot stuff. You look like you're flying. Up against the sky like that. You look like Supergirl.

TRACY: Come over here and look.

KELLY: I don't like heights, remember?

TRACY: Since when?

KELLY: Since childhood.

TRACY: You never told me that.

KELLY: Yes, I did.

TRACY: No, you didn't. Why did we come up here if you're scared of heights?

KELLY: Because you look beautiful framed with sky. Come over here.

(TRACY goes to KELLY. KELLY kisses her and holds the camera out to film the kiss. TRACY notices and pushes the camera away.)

TRACY: Don't!

KELLY: Why not?

TRACY: Because. It will get stolen from your car. End up on the internet. My mom will be watching a TV special on internet porn and there I'll be on the TV screen.

KELLY: Sucking face with some dirty, horny lesbian.

TRACY: And mom will have a heart attack and collapse dead. Face first into a TV dinner.

KELLY: Give me one good shot and I'll stop. A money shot.

TRACY: Get lost, pervert.

KELLY: One shot. It's a small price to pay to shut me up. Please?

TRACY: You're going to erase it, right?

KELLY: Of course I will. We need all the memory for our documentary footage.

TRACY: You're such a liar.

KELLY: Come on.

TRACY: I don't know how you get me to do these things.

(TRACY unbuttons her shirt. She pulls up her sports bra and flashes the camera. Then she laughs, pulls her bra back down and buttons up her shirt.)

KELLY: Sweet. You are so hot.

TRACY: Yeah, whatever. Enjoy. If it ends up on the Internet, I will find you and kill you.

KELLY: Trust me. I'll keep your secret, hot porn star lifestyle just between us.

(KELLY drops the camera into TRACY's backpack. She grabs TRACY and kisses her.)

TRACY: You have such a one track mind.

KELLY: And you love it.

(They make out for a second, then TRACY pulls away.)

TRACY: Hey. Where's the cell phone coverage?

KELLY: What?

TRACY: The area where you can make cell phone calls. You said it was near the drilling site.

KELLY: Yeah.

TRACY: Are we in it?

KELLY: I don't know.

TRACY: I want to call my mom.

KELLY: Now? You want to call her right now?

TRACY: To let her know we got to the village safe. You should call your mother, too.

KELLY: Well, I plan to. But not right now.

(KELLY kisses TRACY again. TRACY pulls away.)

TRACY: Let's just do it while we're thinking about it. So we don't forget.

KELLY: We're going to be surrounded by people for the next two weeks. Jesus, we may not get to be alone again the whole trip. And you want to call your mother? Right now?

TRACY: Yeah.

KELLY: I am going to time this call. No more than one minute.

TRACY: Fine.

KELLY: I'm serious. I will grab the phone out of your hand.

TRACY: I'll probably get the answering machine, anyway. One minute.

(TRACY gets her cell phone from her backpack. She looks at the display. She puts the phone down, disappointed.)

KELLY: Well?

TRACY: No service.

KELLY: Ha! Good.

(KELLY takes the phone and tosses it back into TRACY's backpack.)

TRACY: No. Not good.

(KELLY begins nuzzling TRACY. She gets no response.)

KELLY: What's the matter?

TRACY: I don't know. I just really felt like calling my mom all the sudden. I know she's worried.

KELLY: We'll find the coverage area tomorrow.

TRACY: Okay.

KELLY: You were saying how beautiful it is up here. Right? Isn't that what you were saying when I started filming you?

TRACY: It is beautiful. It's sad though.

KELLY: Why?

TRACY: All those people. Sealing their children into clay pots and throwing them off the cliff. And then walking backwards over the edge. It sounds bad just hearing about it, but being here . . . You can picture it all happening. They must have been crying. The children. The parents probably didn't want to do it, but their chieftain was there and he was watching so they had to. And then they just fell all that way—

KELLY: Archeologists have done digs at the bottom of the cliffs.

TRACY: They have?

KELLY: No one has found any evidence of a mass suicide in the seventeenth century.

TRACY: But you said—

KELLY: Well, it's a story that the U'wa tell. And they believe it happened. Like they believe in Mother Earth the sacred mountain with oil for blood. It's part of their history, their ancestor worship. But it may not be anything more than a story. Don't get too caught up in it.

TRACY: I believe it happened.

KELLY: How come?

TRACY: Because no one would make that up. It's too horrible.

KELLY: Oh, sweetheart. There are lots of people who enjoy making horrible stories. You know that.

(*KELLY kisses her. She puts her hands under TRACY's clothes. TRACY responds. TRACY jumps suddenly and looks out at the jungle.*)

KELLY: *(CONT.)* What?

TRACY: I heard something.

KELLY: It's probably an animal.

TRACY: No. It wasn't.

KELLY: Don't worry about it.

(*KELLY resumes kissing and touching. TRACY is worried.*)

TRACY: Do you think it's the U'wa?

KELLY: I think it's your imagination. Relax. Recite some poetry.

(*TRACY laughs. She relaxes a little.*)

TRACY: I don't know that much. Not by heart.

KELLY: You know the Keats one. From your presentation. That's pretty. Say some of it. You know I think it's sexy when you recite poetry I don't understand.

(*TRACY laughs.*)

TRACY: What part of the poem?

KELLY: Who cares?

TRACY: You asked for a poem. You want the whole poem? Just the sex parts?

KELLY: The end. A short part at the end and then let's get back to business.

TRACY: Such a genuine appreciation for the literature you have. All right. The end.

> *I saw pale kings and princes too,*
> *Pale warriors, death-pale were they all;*
> *They cried - 'La Belle Dame sans Merci*
> *Hath thee in thrall!'*

(A noise or chime. TRACY stops and looks.)

KELLY: It's nothing. Go on.

(KELLY begins to make love to TRACY as she continues.)

TRACY:
> *I saw their starved lips in the gloam,*
> *With horrid warning gaped wide,*
> *And I awoke and found me here,*
> *On the cold hill's side.*
> *And this is why I sojourn here*
> *Alone and palely loitering,--*

(A noise or chime. KELLY and TRACY freeze. Then KELLY rolls so she is on top of TRACY. She covers her with her body and stares into the jungle.)

KELLY: Don't move. Don't attract their attention.

TRACY: It's the U'wa, right?

KELLY: No. They're speaking Spanish. Hush.

TRACY: . . . .

KELLY: . . . .

TRACY: Are they gone?

KELLY: I don't know.

TRACY: What do they want? You think it's the ELN?

KELLY: Probably.

TRACY: What were they saying?

KELLY: My Spanish isn't great. But they said the word Americanas.

TRACY: They're look for us. Why would they do that?

KELLY: I want you to go back to the village. Go north and then circle back to the east. I'll try to draw them back toward the South. I'll make a lot of noise, and they'll follow me.

TRACY: No.

KELLY: Yes. Just do it. Find the cellphone coverage area. Call for help.

TRACY: Don't go. Don't leave me!

KELLY: I love you.

TRACY: I love you, too.

(They kiss. While they kiss, the noise or chime returns. KELLY attempts to run. TRACY grabs her leg and won't let her go.)

KELLY: Tracy! Let me go. I have to go.

TRACY: I don't want them to hurt you.

KELLY: Go to the village! Now! Let go. You have to let me go.

TRACY: I can't. I can't run. I can't breathe. I'm having a panic attack.

(TRACY begins hyperventilating. KELLY cradles her.)

KELLY: Just breathe. Breathe.

TRACY: Don't leave me! . . . I'm scared.

KELLY: I won't leave you. Just breathe. Just breathe.

(The soldiers get closer. They are here.)

7. AND I AWOKE AND FOUND ME HERE

KELLY's apartment.

ELIZABETH: They found you. Alone. On the cliffs.

KELLY: Yes. They raped me first. I told them too. To rape me and leave Tracy alone. They said they would leave her alone. So they cut off my clothes. And two of them held me down. . . . . When it was over they went for Tracy .: . And I fought. . . . The man holding me, I scratched a cheek. And it bled and he swore. And then he let me go. . . . They were cutting Tracy's clothes off and hitting her. And I fought them. . . . I was naked and I didn't have anything to fight with. But I hit them with rocks. And I drove them off her for a second. . . . . Then the leader pulled out a pistol, and he shot me in the leg. . . . . And Tracy screamed. . . . . And I fell. I fell beside her. Close enough to whisper. And I said, "I'm sorry. I'm sorry, Tracy. I love you." . . . . And they dragged me away. And they raped her. . . . They dragged me over to the edge of the cliff and all I could do was watch. . . . I tried to get up. To help her. . . The bullet didn't go through my leg. It tore a chunk off the side of the thigh, so I thought maybe I could get up and go help her. . If the bone wasn't broken, maybe I could walk . . . . And my arm slipped off the edge of the cliff, while I was trying to get up, while I was flailing around and the men laughed. . . . And I had to scramble away from the edge. . . And they were done with Tracy by then, and she was watching me. . . . And she started pleading with the soldiers. To not put me so close to the edge. She told them I was scared of heights. . . . Oh, Tracy. . . . She thought they would care or something . . . . It didn't work out like she hoped. . . . The leader called me a bitch. . . And he said I was probably scared of heights because . . . because I was having a premonición. . . . And then he pushed me off the cliff.

ELIZABETH: . . .

KELLY: I fell backward. I had to twist around to face the cliff wall. . . . And I tried to dig my hands into the cliff side, to break my fall. . . . There are still some scars, see? . . . I was tearing open my hands on rocks. . . .But I did slow the fall a bit. . . And I crashed through some trees, that helped slow me . . . And then there was a ledge . . . I think I was . . . They said afterward that I was about 60 feet down the face of the cliff. And I slammed into the ledge. . . My leg shattered on some rocks. . . .But the rest of the ground was loose dirt. And I survived. . . . It was narrow. About the width of the kitchen counter. . . . Maybe a little wider. . . . I landed on my back. . . . And I passed out from the pain. . . . And then when I came to, I couldn't move. I watched the stars come out. I watched the sun come up. . . . I knew I was dying. And I wanted to. But I didn't know what had happened to Tracy. So I couldn't die. . . I thought she was alive. I thought she was a hostage. . . . So I lived. . . .The U'wa found me the next afternoon. They created a stretcher with some tree branches and a blanket. And hauled me up with ropes. . . . They saved my life. And I thought I was the one going out there to do the saving. . . . Their *Kareka* met me at the top of the cliff. That's like their medicine woman. And priestess. She speaks to their dead ancestors and intercedes on the people's behalf. . . . . It was a miracle that they found me. . . . The soldiers didn't tell them they'd thrown me off the cliff. Tracy was dead and couldn't tell them. And the U'wa chieftain just assumed I was taken hostage and held with the soldiers. . . . But the *Kareka* made the people climb back up to the Cliffs of Glory and spend the night there, praying for me. . . . The people told me that the *Kareka* sat with Tracy's body all night. And she spoke to her spirit. . . .And in the morning, the *Kareka* told the people that Tracy had spoken to her. . . . . And Tracy's spirit said, "On the cold hill's side." Over and over. "On the cold hill's side." Only the *Kareka* could hear her. And so they began searching the cliff side and they found me.

ELIZABETH: . . .

KELLY: They carried me over to her body. I waited with her until they brought the trucks. I held her hand. . . . The soldiers had shot her in the head.

ELIZABETH: . . .

KELLY: . . .

ELIZABETH: Do you have any idea why?

KELLY: *(makes a small noise)* . . .

ELIZABETH: Do you think she fought them?

KELLY: . . .

ELIZABETH: Do you know how long she lived, after you were pushed?

KELLY: . . .

ELIZABETH: If she was tortured?

KELLY: . . .

ELIZABETH: I'd better go. I'll miss my flight. And you'll miss your dinner plans.

KELLY: . . .

ELIZABETH: If you think of anything else. Send me an email.

KELLY: Okay.

ELIZABETH: The rain hasn't let up, I see. If anything it's gotten worse. Story of my life.

KELLY: I don't really have dinner plans.

ELIZABETH: . . .

KELLY: You could stay here. Until the rain lets up.

ELIZABETH: No, thank you.

KELLY: You could call your husband, and tell him you're taking a later flight.

ELIZABETH: He can't get on very well without me. He has trouble sleeping if I'm not with him.

KELLY: Oh.

ELIZABETH: So I should get back.

KELLY: . . .

ELIZABETH: I hope you don't kill yourself. It will break your mother's heart. You're young. You'll find somebody else to love.

KELLY: I thought you didn't believe we were in love. It was demons that brought us together, or two poetries, or something. Right? Not love.

ELIZABETH: Well.

KELLY: . . .

ELIZABETH: I don't approve of the relationship. I know that's not what you want to hear. But I wish it had never happened.

KELLY: Okay.

ELIZABETH: But, I do think . . . as much as anybody can be in love in this world, you were in love with my daughter. . . . That still doesn't mean I approve. It doesn't mean that I don't wish you had never been born. And for Tracy's part, I still hope she didn't love you. . . . But . . . I . . . imagine she did.

KELLY: Thank you.

ELIZABETH: . . .

KELLY: . . .

ELIZABETH: Well, I'll be glad to get back to Chicago. It will be drier. Possibly warmer. Bill will be disappointed that I didn't get to the beach.

KELLY: Maybe next time you visit.

ELIZABETH: Oh, I don't think I'll be back this way any-time soon.

KELLY: No.

ELIZABETH: I'll look for your email. And the photos.

(ELIZABETH gathers up her handbag and the plastic wrapped backpack. She goes to the door.)

KELLY: Wait.

ELIZABETH: . . .

KELLY: . . . . There's something else. There's something else of hers. That I didn't tell you about.

(KELLY goes to her desk and takes the MP3 player from the desk drawer. She brings it to ELIZABETH.)

KELLY: *(CONT.)* I was recording. With the digital camera. Just before the soldiers found us. And I put it in Tracy's backpack. I forgot to turn it off. So it was recording the whole time. . . . There's no picture, because it was in Tracy's bag. . . . But you can hear everything. . . . If you want . . . And maybe you don't want, because it's really hard to listen to it . . . but if you want, you can hear what happened after they pushed me. . . . You can hear what she said. And you can hear them kill her.

ELIZABETH: This thing . . . this little machine . . . does all that?

KELLY: I put the sound on my computer. I made an MP3 file. I loaded it. It starts right after they push me off the cliff. I don't know if you want to hear it.

ELIZABETH: You can hear Tracy?

KELLY: Yes.

ELIZABETH: How?

KELLY: You press this button.

(ELIZABETH puts down her handbag and the backpack. She takes the MP3 player.)

ELIZABETH: How long is the recording?

KELLY: About a minute.

(ELIZABETH puts the earphones on her head. She walks over to the window. She hesitates. She stands there in suspense.

She pushes the button.

TRACY appears outside the window. She is naked. Her nose is bleeding and her body is bruised. She rushes to the window.)

TRACY: Murderers! Bastards! . . . She was good! . . . I loved her! . . . We're here to protect. Protect blood from drilling. Protect children from clay pots. Protect people from walking backwards. Protect you. We're good. You bastards! Murderers! You're wrong! What you did-- you should die for it! I should kill you. Bite through your skin and tear off your face!

(She bangs on the glass.)

I will fight! I will fight! I will fight you! And I will win! I will defeat you! People don't do this and stay people! You'll be sleeping one night and I'll come for you! I'll come with knives and cut your eyelids off so you watch me kill you! I'll be cruel and I'll be strong!

You'll never get rid of me! Not until I've killed you. I'll find you. I'll hunt you. I'll keep coming back! Until you walk off that cliff one by one. This was wrong and I was here to see it! Murderers! Evil! Filth! Bastards! Rapists! The women who gave you life should be ashamed! They should take that gift back! Your mothers should find you and kill you! They should hunt you like animals with spears and with arrows! They should spit in your faces as they correct their mistakes and open your worthless throats!

I won't be quiet! I'll follow you wherever you go! I will find where you live! I won't stop telling people what you did! Your neighbors will know you're a murderer and a rapist! Your sisters will know! Your fathers will know! Your mothers will know! Your priests will know! Stray dogs in the streets of your town will know! I won't stop telling people until the world knows!

Until there is not a shack, a hovel, a cave or hole on the planet you can crawl into without someone knowing! I will keep telling and telling and telling! You'll have to kill me! I'll come for you in the night with razors! With stones! With my bared teeth on your throat!--

(TRACY is shot in the back of the head. The window is drenched in an explosion of blood. She falls. ELIZABETH jumps hearing the gunshot and rips the earplugs

*from her ears. She puts her hands to her mouth. ELIZA-
BETH and KELLY stare at the bloody window.)*

ELIZABETH: . . .

KELLY: . . .

ELIZABETH: . . .

KELLY: . . .

ELIZABETH: . . .

KELLY: . . .

*(ELIZABETH moans. She falls to her knees and cries.
KELLY kneels at her side and holds her.)*

ELIZABETH: Oh . . . . Tracy. Oh, Tracy . . . .

KELLY: I know. I know.

ELIZABETH: Oh. Oh.

*(KELLY rocks her back and forth, making a soothing,
shushing sound.*

*After a long moment, ELIZABETH gently pulls herself
out of KELLY's embrace. They sit for a moment, looking
at one another.*

*ELIZABETH finds the MP3 player on the floor and
hands it to KELLY.)*

KELLY: Would you like a copy of this?

ELIZABETH: . . .

KELLY: . . .

ELIZABETH: No.

KELLY: Okay.

ELIZABETH: I'd better get going. I have to get the rental car back. Catch the plane.

KELLY: It's really coming down hard out there.

ELIZABETH: I see.

KELLY: And the wind is picking up.

ELIZABETH: It's been rattling the glass in the window.

KELLY: I don't think it's going to stop anytime soon.

ELIZABETH: No, I don't think it will.

KELLY: . . .

ELIZABETH: . . .

KELLY: Are you sure you don't want to stay here?

ELIZABETH: No. No, thank you.

KELLY: . . .

ELIZABETH: . . .

KELLY: Okay.

(ELIZABETH takes her handbag and the plastic wrapped backpack. She opens the door. She puts on her orange poncho and opens her umbrella. She looks back at KELLY.)

ELIZABETH: . . .

KELLY: . . .

(ELIZABETH exits. KELLY stands in the doorway and watches until ELIZABETH has left the courtyard. We hear a metal security gate slam shut.

KELLY goes back inside. She closes the door and locks it. She puts the MP3 player earplugs in her ears. She goes to the couch and climbs onto it, curling her body around TRACY's clothes. She has to use two hands to maneuver her bad leg into place. She positions herself as if she were embracing TRACY's body. She pushes play on the MP3 player and listens.

After a moment, she unfastens her jeans and touches herself softly.

End play.)

Also Available From
Johnna Adams

Synopsis: Doug and Cheryl are horrible single parents drawn together by their equally horrible daughters. The star-crossed parental units journey from first meeting to first date, to first time, to first joint parent-teacher meeting, to proposal and more. They attempt to form a modern nuclear family while living in perpetual fear of the fruit of their loins and someone abducting young girls in their town.

Cast Size: 1 Male, 1 Female

"Stunning"
- Las Vegas Weekly

"Highly entertaining"
- Las Vegas Review Journal

NOTES

NOTES

NOTES

NOTES

Made in the USA
San Bernardino, CA
20 June 2014